Blankets & Booties

These six blanket-and-bootie sets for Baby will tempt you to crochet them all, and why not, when they make such welcome shower gifts? From rows of hearts to puff stitches that form the symbols for hugs and kisses, each blanket offers something special. Pretty stripes, buds & blooms, leaf clusters, and a textured latticework—the pretty patterns are echoed whenever possible on the soft booties. With these darling designs to crochet, you have the best way to pamper tiny tykes right down to their adorable toes!

LEISURE ARTS, INC.
Maumelle, Arkansas

Little Boy Blue

Shown on page 5.

 INTERMEDIATE

MATERIALS

Light Weight Yarn
[5 ounces, 468 yards
(140 grams, 429 meters) per skein]:
  Blanket - 4 skeins
  Booties - 75 yards (68.5 meters)
Crochet hook as indicated below **or**
size needed for gauge
  Blanket
    Size F (3.75 mm)
  Booties
    0 to 3 months - size E (3.5 mm)
    3 to 6 months - size F (3.75 mm)
¹/₄"w (7 mm) Ribbon - 32" (81.5 cm) length
Yarn needle

GAUGES
Blanket
In pattern, 16 dc and 8 rows = 4" (10 cm)
Booties
0 to 3 months - 7 dc = 1¹/₂" (3.75 cm)
3 to 6 months - 6 dc = 1¹/₂" (3.75 cm)

GAUGE SWATCHES
Blanket: 4¹/₄"w x 4"h (10.75 cm x 10 cm)
Ch 19.
Work same as Blanket Body for 8 rows.
Finish off.

Booties
  0 to 3 months - Approximately 3³/₄" (9.5 cm)
  3 to 6 months - Approximately 4" (10 cm)
Work same as Sole.

STITCH GUIDE

FRONT POST DOUBLE CROCHET
  (abbreviated FPdc)
YO, insert hook from **front** to **back** around post of st indicated *(Fig. 4, page 30)*, YO and pull up a loop (3 loops on hook), (YO and draw through 2 loops on hook) twice. Skip st behind FPdc.

BACK POST DOUBLE CROCHET
  (abbreviated BPdc)
YO, insert hook from **back** to **front** around post of FPdc indicated *(Fig. 4, page 30)*, YO and pull up a loop (3 loops on hook), (YO and draw through 2 loops on hook) twice. Skip st in front of BPdc.

FRONT POST CLUSTER
  (abbreviated FP Cluster)
★ YO, insert hook from **front** to **back** around post of st indicated *(Fig. 4, page 30)*, YO and pull up a loop, YO and draw through 2 loops on hook; repeat from ★ once **more**, YO and draw through all 3 loops on hook. Skip st behind FP Cluster.

BLANKET

Finished Size: 35" x 48½" (89 cm x 123 cm)

BODY

Ch 127, place a marker in third ch from hook for st placement.

Row 1: Dc in fourth ch from hook **(3 skipped chs count as first dc)** and in each ch across: 125 dc.

Row 2 (Right side)**:** Ch 3 **(counts as first dc, now and throughout)**, turn; dc in next 4 dc, ★ work FPdc around next dc, dc in next 2 dc, work FP Cluster around next dc, dc in next 2 dc, work FPdc around next dc, dc in next 5 dc; repeat from ★ across: 95 dc, 20 FPdc, and 10 FP Clusters.

Note: Loop a short piece of yarn around any stitch to mark Row 2 as **right** side.

Row 3: Ch 3, turn; dc in next 4 dc, (work BPdc around next FPdc, dc in next 5 sts) across: 105 dc and 20 BPdc.

Row 4: Ch 3, turn; dc in next dc, work FP Cluster around next dc, dc in next 2 dc, ★ work FPdc around next BPdc, dc in next 5 dc, work FPdc around next BPdc, dc in next 2 dc, work FP Cluster around next dc, dc in next 2 dc; repeat from ★ across: 94 dc, 20 FPdc, and 11 FP Clusters.

Row 5: Ch 3, turn; dc in next 4 sts, (work BPdc around next FPdc, dc in next 5 sts) across: 105 dc and 20 BPdc.

Row 6: Ch 3, turn; dc in next 4 dc, ★ work FPdc around next BPdc, dc in next 2 dc, work FP Cluster around next dc, dc in next 2 dc, work FPdc around next BPdc, dc in next 5 dc; repeat from ★ across: 95 dc, 20 FPdc, and 10 FP Clusters.

Repeat Rows 3-6 for pattern until Body measures approximately 44½" (113 cm) from beginning ch, ending by working a **wrong** side row; do **not** finish off.

EDGING

Rnd 1 (Right side)**:** Ch 3, turn; (2 dc, ch 1, 3 dc) in first dc, dc in each st across to last dc, (3 dc, ch 1, 3 dc) in last dc; work 177 dc evenly spaced across end of rows; working in free loops of beginning ch *(Fig. 2b, page 30)*, (3 dc, ch 1, 3 dc) in marked ch, dc in each ch across to last ch, (3 dc, ch 1, 3 dc) in last ch; work 177 dc evenly spaced across end of rows; join with slip st to first dc: 624 dc and 4 ch-1 sps.

Rnd 2: Ch 3, do **not** turn; skip next dc, work FP Cluster around next dc, ch 3, skip next corner ch-1 sp, work FP Cluster around next dc, ★ skip next dc, dc in next 5 dc, (work FP Cluster around next dc, dc in next 5 dc) across to within 2 dc of next corner ch-1 sp, skip next dc, work FP Cluster around next dc, ch 3, skip next corner ch-1 sp, work FP Cluster around next dc; repeat from ★ 2 times **more**, skip next dc, (dc in next 5 dc, work FP Cluster around next dc) across to last 4 dc, dc in last 4 dc; join with slip st to first dc: 510 dc, 106 FP Clusters, and 4 ch-3 sps.

Rnd 3: Slip st in next FP Cluster and in next corner ch-3 sp, ch 3, (2 dc, ch 1, 3 dc) in same sp, work FP Cluster around next FP Cluster, skip next dc, dc in next 3 dc, ★ † skip next dc, work (FP Cluster, ch 3, FP Cluster) around next FP Cluster, skip next dc, dc in next 3 dc †; repeat from † to † across to within 2 sts of next corner ch-3 sp, skip next dc, work FP Cluster around next FP Cluster, (3 dc, ch 1, 3 dc) in next corner ch-3 sp, work FP Cluster around next FP Cluster, skip next dc, dc in next 3 dc; repeat from ★ 2 times **more**, then repeat from † to † across to last 2 sts, skip next st, work FP Cluster around last FP Cluster; join with slip st to first dc: 330 dc, 204 FP Clusters, and 102 sps.

Rnd 4: Ch 1, **turn**; sc in same st as joining and in each st around, working 3 sc in each ch-3 sp and one sc in each ch-1 sp; join with slip st to first sc, finish off.

Instructions continued on page 4.

BOOTIES
SOLE

Ch 13.

Rnd 1 (Right side): 3 Sc in second ch from hook, sc in next 10 chs, 5 sc in last ch; working in free loops of beginning ch **(Fig. 2b, page 30)**, sc in next 10 chs, 2 sc in next ch; join with slip st to Back Loop Only of first sc **(Fig. 3, page 30)**: 30 sc.

Note: Loop a short piece of yarn around any stitch to mark Rnd 1 as **right** side.

Rnd 2: Ch 3 **(counts as first dc, now and throughout unless otherwise indicated)**, working in Back Loops Only, 2 dc in next sc, hdc in next 3 sc, sc in next 4 sc, hdc in next 4 sc, 2 dc in each of next 2 sc, dc in next sc, 2 dc in each of next 2 sc, hdc in next 4 sc, sc in next 4 sc, hdc in next 3 sc, 2 dc in next sc; join with slip st to first dc, do **not** finish off: 36 sts.

SIDES

Rnd 1: Ch 3, dc in Back Loop Only of next st and each st around; join with slip st **both** loops of first dc.

Rnd 2: Ch 3, working in both loops, dc in next dc, work FP Cluster around next dc, dc in next 2 dc, work FPdc around next dc, ★ dc in next 2 dc, work FP Cluster around next dc, dc in next 2 dc, work FPdc around next dc; repeat from ★ around; join with slip st to first dc: 24 dc, 6 FPdc, and 6 FP Clusters.

To decrease (uses next 2 sts), ★ YO, insert hook in **next** st, YO and pull up a loop, YO and draw through 2 loops on hook; repeat from ★ once **more**, YO and draw through all 3 loops on hook **(counts as one dc)**.

Rnd 3: Ch 1, sc in same st as joining and in next 13 sts, decrease, (dc in next dc, decrease) 3 times, sc in last 11 sts; join with slip st to first sc: 32 sts.

Rnd 4: Ch 1, sc in same st as joining and in next 13 sc, decrease 4 times, sc in last 10 sc; join with slip st to first sc, do **not** finish off: 28 sts.

CUFF

Rnd 1 (Eyelet rnd): Ch 3 **(counts as first hdc plus ch 1)**, skip next st, (hdc in next st, ch 1, skip next st) 5 times, (dc in next st, ch 1, skip next st) 5 times, (hdc in next st, ch 1, skip next st) 3 times; join with slip st to first hdc: 14 ch-1 sps.

Rnd 2: Ch 1, sc in same st as joining, 2 sc in each of next 7 ch-1 sps, sc in next dc, 2 sc in each of next 7 ch-1 sps; join with slip st to first sc: 30 sc.

Rnd 3: Ch 3, dc in next sc and in each sc around; join with slip st to first dc.

Rnd 4: Ch 3, dc in next 2 dc, skip next dc, work (FP Cluster, ch 3, FP Cluster) around next dc, skip next dc, ★ dc in next 3 dc, skip next dc, work (FP Cluster, ch 3, FP Cluster) around next dc, skip next dc; repeat from ★ around; join with slip st to first dc: 15 dc, 10 FP Clusters, and 5 ch-3 sps.

Rnd 5: Ch 1, **turn**; sc in next FP Cluster, 3 sc in next ch-3 sp, (sc in next 5 sts, 3 sc in next ch-3 sp) around to last 4 sts, sc in last 4 sts; join with slip st to first sc, finish off.

Beginning at center front, weave a 16" (40.5 cm) length of ribbon through Eyelet rnd.

Mint Delight

Shown on page 9.

◼◼◼◻ **INTERMEDIATE**

MATERIALS

Light Weight Yarn  **LIGHT 3**

[5 ounces, 468 yards
(140 grams, 429 meters) per skein]:
  Blanket - 5 skeins
  Booties - 65 yards (59.5 meters)
Crochet hook as indicated below **or**
  size needed for gauge
  Blanket
    Size F (3.75 mm)
  Booties
    0 to 3 months - size E (3.5 mm)
    3 to 6 months - size F (3.75 mm)
$^1/_4$"w (7 mm) Ribbon - 32" (81.5 cm) length
Yarn needle

GAUGES

Blanket
In pattern, 19 sts and 12 rows = $4^3/_4$" (12 cm)
Booties
0 to 3 months - 7 dc = $1^1/_2$" (3.75 cm)
3 to 6 months - 6 dc = $1^1/_2$" (3.75 cm)

GAUGE SWATCHES

Blanket: $4^1/_4$"w x $4^3/_4$"h (10.75 cm x 12 cm)
Ch 18.
Work same as Body for 12 rows.
Finish off.

Booties

  0 to 3 months - Approximately $3^3/_4$" (9.5 cm)
  3 to 6 months - Approximately 4" (10 cm)
Work same as Sole.

STITCH GUIDE

BEGINNING CLUSTER (uses one st)
★ YO, insert hook in st indicated, YO and pull up a loop, YO and draw through 2 loops on hook; repeat from ★ once **more**, YO and draw through all 3 loops on hook.
CLUSTER (uses one sc)
★ YO, insert hook in sc indicated, YO and pull up a loop, YO and draw through 2 loops on hook; repeat from ★ 2 times **more**, YO and draw through all 4 loops on hook.

BLANKET

Finished Size: $37^3/_4$" x 52" (96 cm x 132 cm)

BODY

Ch 138.

Row 1: Sc in second ch from hook and in each ch across: 137 sc.

Row 2 (Right side)**:** Ch 3 **(counts as first dc, now and throughout)**, turn; dc in next sc and in each sc across.

Note: Loop a short piece of yarn around any stitch to mark Row 2 as **right** side.

Row 3: Ch 1, turn; sc in each dc across.

Row 4: Ch 3, turn; dc in next 2 sc, ch 1, skip next sc, work Cluster in next sc, ch 1, ★ skip next sc, dc in next 5 sc, ch 1, skip next sc, work Cluster in next sc, ch 1; repeat from ★ across to last 4 sc, skip next sc, dc in last 3 sc: 86 dc, 17 Clusters, and 34 ch-1 sps.

Row 5: Ch 1, turn; sc in first 3 dc and in next ch-1 sp, sc in next Cluster and in next ch-1 sp, ★ sc in next 5 dc and in next ch-1 sp, sc in next Cluster and in next ch-1 sp; repeat from ★ across to last 3 dc, sc in last 3 dc: 137 sc.

Row 6: Ch 3, turn; dc in next sc, skip next 2 sc, work Cluster in next sc, (ch 2, work Cluster in same st) twice, ★ skip next 3 sc, 3 dc in next sc, skip next 3 sc, work Cluster in next sc, (ch 2, work Cluster in same st) twice; repeat from ★ across to last 4 sc, skip next 2 sc, dc in last 2 sc: 52 dc, 51 Clusters, and 34 ch-2 sps.

Row 7: Ch 3, turn; dc in next dc, 2 sc in next ch-2 sp, sc in next Cluster, 2 sc in next ch-2 sp, ★ skip next Cluster and next dc, 3 dc in next dc, 2 sc in next ch-2 sp, sc in next Cluster, 2 sc in next ch-2 sp; repeat from ★ across to last 3 sts, skip next Cluster, dc in last 2 dc: 85 sc and 52 dc.

Row 8: Ch 3, turn; dc in next st and in each st across: 137 dc.

Repeat Rows 3-8 for pattern, until Body measures approximately 48¹/₂" (123 cm) from beginning ch, ending by working Row 3; do **not** finish off.

EDGING

Rnd 1: Ch 1, do **not** turn; with **wrong** side facing, work 193 sc evenly spaced across end of rows; working in free loops of beginning ch *(Fig. 2b, page 30)*, 3 sc in first ch, work 133 sc evenly spaced across to last ch, 3 sc in last ch; work 193 sc evenly spaced across end of rows; working in sts across last row, 3 sc in first sc, work 133 sc evenly spaced across to last sc, 3 sc in last sc; join with slip st to first sc: 664 sc.

Rnd 2: Ch 3, turn; dc in next sc, 5 dc in next sc, ★ dc in each sc across to center sc of next corner 3-sc group, 5 dc in corner sc; repeat from ★ 2 times **more**, dc in each sc across; join with slip st to first dc: 680 dc.

Rnd 3: Ch 1, turn; sc in same st as joining and in each dc across to center dc of next corner 5-dc group, 3 sc in center dc, ★ sc in each dc across to center dc of next corner 5-dc group, 3 sc in center dc; repeat from ★ 2 times **more**, sc in last 3 dc; join with slip st to first sc: 688 sc.

Rnd 4: Ch 3, turn; work Beginning Cluster in same st as joining, (ch 2, work Cluster in same st) twice, skip next 2 sc, dc in next sc, skip next sc, work Cluster in next corner sc, (ch 2, work Cluster in same st) twice, skip next sc, dc in next sc, ★ † skip next 2 sc, work Cluster in next sc, (ch 2, work Cluster in same st) twice, skip next 2 sc, dc in next sc †, repeat from † to † across to within one sc of next corner sc, skip next sc, work Cluster in corner sc, (ch 2, work Cluster in same st) twice, skip next sc, dc in next sc; repeat from ★ 2 times **more**, skip next 2 sc, [work Cluster in next sc, (ch 2, work Cluster in same st) twice, skip next 2 sc, dc in next sc, skip next 2 sc] across; join with slip st to top of Beginning Cluster.

Rnd 5: Ch 1, turn; ★ slip st in next dc, 3 sc in next ch-2 sp, sc in next Cluster, 3 sc in next ch-2 sp; repeat from ★ around; join with slip st to first slip st, finish off.

BOOTIES
SOLE
Ch 13.

Rnd 1 (Right side)**:** 3 Sc in second ch from hook, sc in next 10 chs, 5 sc in last ch; working in free loops of beginning ch *(Fig. 2b, page 30)*, sc in next 10 chs, 2 sc in next ch; join with slip st to Back Loop Only of first sc *(Fig. 3, page 30)*: 30 sc.

Note: Loop a short piece of yarn around any stitch to mark Rnd 1 as **right** side.

Instructions continued on page 8.

Rnd 2: Ch 3 **(counts as first dc, now and throughout unless otherwise indicated)**, working in Back Loops Only, 2 dc in next sc, hdc in next 3 sc, sc in next 4 sc, hdc in next 3 sc, dc in next sc, (2 dc in each of next 2 sc, dc in next sc) twice, hdc in next 3 sc, sc in next 4 sc, hdc in next 3 sc, 2 dc in next sc; join with slip st to first dc, do **not** finish off: 36 sts.

SIDES

Rnd 1: Ch 1, **turn**; sc in Front Loop Only of same st as joining *(Fig. 3, page 30)* and each st around; join with slip st to **both** loops of first sc.

Rnd 2: Ch 3, turn; dc in both loops of next sc and each sc around; join with slip st to first dc.

To single crochet decrease (abbreviated sc decrease), pull up a loop in each of next 2 dc, YO and draw through all 3 loops on hook **(counts as one sc)**.

Rnd 3: Ch 1, turn; sc in first 12 dc, sc decrease, (sc in next 2 dc, sc decrease) 3 times, sc in last 10 dc; join with slip st to first sc: 32 sc.

To double crochet decrease (abbreviated dc decrease) (uses next 2 sc), ★ YO, insert hook in **next** sc, YO and pull up a loop, YO and draw through 2 loops on hook; repeat from ★ once **more**, YO and draw through all 3 loops on hook **(counts as one dc)**.

Rnd 4: Ch 3, turn; dc in next 11 sc, dc decrease 4 times, dc in last 12 sc; join with slip st to first dc: 28 dc.

Rnd 5: Ch 1, turn; sc in each dc around; join with slip st to first sc.

CUFF

Rnd 1 (Eyelet rnd)**:** Ch 3 **(counts as first hdc plus ch 1)**, turn; skip next sc, (hdc in next sc, ch 1, skip next sc) 4 times, (dc in next sc, ch 1, skip next sc) 4 times, (hdc in next sc, ch 1, skip next sc) 5 times; join with slip st to first hdc: 14 ch-1 sps.

Rnd 2: Ch 1, turn; sc in same st as joining, 2 sc in each of next 7 ch-1 sps, sc in next dc, 2 sc in each of next 7 ch-1 sps; join with slip st to first sc: 30 sc.

Rnd 3: Ch 3, turn; dc in next sc and in each sc around; join with slip st to first dc.

Rnd 4: Ch 1, turn; sc in each dc around; join with slip st to first sc.

Rnd 5: Ch 3, turn; skip next 2 sc, work Cluster in next sc, (ch 2, work Cluster in same st) twice, skip next 2 sc, ★ dc in next sc, skip next 2 sc, work Cluster in next sc, (ch 2, work Cluster in same st) twice, skip next 2 sc; repeat from ★ around; join with slip st to first dc.

Rnd 6: Ch 1, turn; ★ 3 sc in next ch-2 sp, sc in next Cluster, 3 sc in next ch-2 sp, skip next Cluster, slip st in next dc; repeat from ★ around; join with slip st to first sc, finish off.

Beginning at center front, weave a 16" (40.5 cm) length of ribbon through Eyelet rnd.

Serenity Stripes

Shown on page 13.

 INTERMEDIATE

MATERIALS

Light Weight Yarn
[3.5 ounces, 359 yards
(100 grams, 328 meters) per skein]:

Blanket
   Green - 4 skeins
   Yellow - 2 skeins
   White - 1 skein
Booties
   Green - 50 yards (45.5 meters)
   Yellow - 15 yards (13.5 meters)
   White - 10 yards (9 meters)
Crochet hook as indicated below **or**
size needed for gauge
Blanket
   Size F (3.75 mm)
Booties
   0 to 3 months - size E (3.5 mm)
   3 to 6 months - size F (3.75 mm)
$^1/_4$"w (7 mm) Ribbon - 32" (81.5 cm) length
Yarn needle

GAUGES
Blanket
In pattern, (2 sc, ch 2) 4 times and
14 rows = $2^1/_2$" (6.25 cm)
Booties
0 to 3 months - 8 dc = $1^1/_2$" (3.75 cm)
3 to 6 months - 7 dc = $1^1/_2$" (3.75 cm)

GAUGE SWATCHES
Blanket: $2^7/_8$" (7.25 cm) square
With Green, ch 19.
Work same as Blanket for 16 rows.
Finish off.

Booties
   0 to 3 months - Approximately $3^3/_4$" (9.5 cm)
   3 to 6 months - Approximately 4" (10 cm)
Work same as Sole.

BLANKET
Finished Size: 35" x 45" (89 cm x 114.5 cm)

Each row is worked across the length of the Blanket.
When joining yarn and finishing off, always leave an
8" (20.5 cm) end to be worked into fringe.

BODY
With Green, ch 287.

Row 1: Working in back ridge of chs *(Fig. 1, page 30)*
sc in second ch from hook and in next ch, ★ ch 2, skip
next 2 chs, sc in next 2 chs; repeat from ★ across:
144 sc and 71 ch-2 sps.

Row 2 (Right side)**:** Ch 1, turn; sc in first 2 sc,
(ch 2, sc in next 2 sc) across.

Note: Loop a short piece of yarn around any stitch
to mark Row 2 as **right** side.

Rows 3 and 4: Ch 1, turn; sc in first 2 sc, (ch 2, sc in next 2 sc) across; at end of last row, finish off.

Row 5: With **wrong** side facing, join Yellow with sc in first sc *(see Joining With Sc, page 30)*; sc in next sc, (ch 2, sc in next 2 sc) across; finish off.

Row 6: With **right** side facing, join Green with sc in first sc; sc in next sc, (ch 2, sc in next 2 sc) across; finish off.

Row 7: With **wrong** side facing, join White with sc in first sc; sc in next sc, (ch 2, sc in next 2 sc) across; finish off.

Row 8: With **right** side facing, join Green with sc in first sc; sc in next sc, (ch 2, sc in next 2 sc) across; finish off.

Row 9: With **wrong** side facing, join Yellow with sc in first sc; sc in next sc, (ch 2, sc in next 2 sc) across; finish off.

Row 10: With **right** side facing, join Green with sc in first sc; sc in next sc, (ch 2, sc in next 2 sc) across; do **not** finish off.

Rows 11 and 12: Ch 1, turn; sc in first 2 sc, (ch 2, sc in next 2 sc) across; at end of last row, finish off.

Row 13: With **wrong** side facing, join Yellow with sc in first sc; sc in next sc, (ch 2, sc in next 2 sc) across; do **not** finish off.

Rows 14 and 15: Ch 1, turn; sc in first 2 sc, (ch 2, sc in next 2 sc) across; at end of last row, finish off.

Row 16: With **right** side facing, join Green with sc in first sc; sc in next sc, (ch 2, sc in next 2 sc) across; do **not** finish off.

Rows 17-192: Repeat Rows 3-16, 12 times; then repeat Rows 3-10 once **more**.

Rows 193-195: Ch 1, turn; sc in first 2 sc, (ch 2, sc in next 2 sc) across; at end of last row, finish off.

Cut a piece of cardboard 3" (7.5 cm) wide and 8" (20.5 cm) long. Wind the yarn **loosely** and **evenly** lengthwise around the cardboard until the card is filled, then cut across one end; repeat as needed. Fold one strand of corresponding color yarn in half. With **wrong** side facing and using a crochet hook, draw the folded end up through end of first row and pull the loose ends through the folded end *(Fig. A)*; draw the knot up tightly *(Fig. B)*. Repeat in end of each row across short edges with corresponding color. Lay flat on a hard surface and trim the ends.

Fig. A

Fig. B

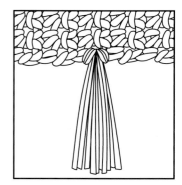

BOOTIES
SOLE
With Green, ch 14.

Rnd 1 (Right side)**:** 2 Dc in fourth ch from hook **(3 skipped chs count as first dc)**, dc in next 3 chs, hdc in next 3 chs, dc in next 3 chs, 7 dc in last ch; working in free loops of beginning ch *(Fig. 2b, page 30)*, dc in next 3 chs, hdc in next 3 chs, dc in next 3 chs, 2 dc in next ch; join with slip st to first dc: 30 sts.

Note: Loop a short piece of yarn around any stitch to mark Rnd 1 as **right** side.

Rnd 2: Ch 3 **(counts as first dc, now and throughout)**, 2 dc in each of next 2 dc, 2 hdc in next dc, hdc in next 6 sts, dc in next 2 dc, 2 dc in each of next 3 dc, dc in next dc, 2 dc in each of next 3 dc, dc in next 2 dc, hdc in next 6 sts, 2 hdc in next dc, 2 dc in each of last 2 dc; join with slip st to first dc: 42 sts.

Instructions continued on page 12.

SIDES

Rnd 1: Ch 1, working in Back Loops Only **(Fig. 3, page 30)**, sc in same st as joining and in each st around; join with slip st to **both** loops first sc, finish off.

Rnd 2: With **wrong** side facing and working in both loops, join Yellow with sc in same st as joining **(see Joining With Sc, page 30)**; ch 2, skip next 2 sc, (sc in next 2 sc, ch 2, skip next 2 sc) twice, sc in next 20 sc, ch 2, skip next 2 sc, (sc in next 2 sc, ch 2, skip next 2 sc) twice, sc in last sc; join with slip st to first sc, finish off: 30 sc and 6 ch-2 sps.

Rnd 3: With **right** side facing, join Green with sc in same st as joining; sc in next sc, ch 2, (sc in next 2 sc, ch 2) twice, sc in next 20 sc, ch 2, (sc in next 2 sc, ch 2) twice; join with slip st to first sc, finish off.

Rnd 4: With **wrong** side facing, join White with sc in same st as joining; ch 2, (sc in next 2 sc, ch 2) twice, sc in next 20 sc, ch 2, (sc in next 2 sc, ch 2) twice, sc in last sc; join with slip st to first sc, finish off.

To decrease (uses next 2 sc), ★ YO, insert hook in **next** sc, YO and pull up a loop, YO and draw through 2 loops on hook; repeat from ★ once **more**, YO and draw through all 3 loops on hook **(counts as one dc)**.

Rnd 5: With **right** side facing, join Green with sc in same st as joining; sc in next sc, (ch 2, sc in next 2 sc) 3 times, dc in next sc, decrease 7 times, dc in next sc, (sc in next 2 sc, ch 2) 3 times; join with slip st to first sc, finish off: 23 sts and 6 ch-2 sps.

Rnd 6: With **wrong** side facing, join Yellow with sc in same st as joining; ch 2, (sc in next 2 sc, ch 2) twice, sc in next 13 sts, ch 2, (sc in next 2 sc, ch 2) twice, sc in last sc; join with slip st to first sc, finish off.

Rnd 7: With **right** side facing, join Green with sc in same st as joining; sc in next sc, ch 2, (sc in next 2 sc, ch 2) twice, sc in next 6 sc, [pull up a loop in each of next 2 sc, YO and draw through all 3 loops on hook **(counts as one sc)**], sc in next 5 sc, ch 2, (sc in next 2 sc, ch 2) twice; join with slip st to first sc, do **not** finish off: 22 sts and 6 ch-2 sps.

CUFF

Rnd 1 (Eyelet rnd)**:** Ch 3 **(counts as first hdc plus ch 1)**, do **not** turn; [hdc in next ch-2 sp, ch 1, hdc in next sc, ch 1] 3 times, skip next sc, (hdc in next sc, ch 1, skip next sc) 5 times, hdc in next ch-2 sp, ch 1, [hdc in next sc, ch 1, hdc in next ch-2 sp, ch 1] twice; join with slip st to first hdc: 17 ch-1 sps.

Rnd 2: Ch 1, 2 sc in each of next 4 ch-1 sps, 3 sc in next ch-1 sp, 2 sc in each of next 8 ch-1 sps, 3 sc in next ch-1 sp, 2 sc in each of last 3 ch-1 sps; join with slip st to first sc, finish off: 36 sc.

Rnd 3: With **wrong** side facing, join Yellow with sc in same st as joining; ch 2, ★ skip next 2 sc, sc in next 2 sc, ch 2; repeat from ★ around to last 3 sc, skip next 2 sc, sc in last sc; join with slip st to first sc, finish off: 18 sc and 9 ch-2 sps.

Rnd 4: With **right** side facing, join Green with sc in same st as joining; sc in next sc, ch 2, (sc in next 2 sc, ch 2) around; join with slip st to first sc, finish off.

Rnd 5: With **wrong** side facing, join White with sc in same st as joining; ch 2, (sc in next 2 sc, ch 2) around to last sc, sc in last sc; join with slip st to first sc, finish off.

Rnd 6: With **right** side facing, join Green with sc in same st as joining; sc in next sc, ch 2, (sc in next 2 sc, ch 2) around; join with slip st to first sc, finish off.

Rnd 7: With **wrong** side facing, join Yellow with sc in same st as joining; ch 2, (sc in next 2 sc, ch 2) around to last sc, sc in last sc; join with slip st to first sc, finish off.

Rnd 8: With **right** side facing, join Green with sc in same st as joining; sc in next sc, ch 2, (sc in next 2 sc, ch 2) around; join with slip st to first sc, finish off.

Beginning at center front, weave a 16" (40.5 cm) length of ribbon through Eyelet rnd.

Sweet Hugs & Kisses

Shown on page 17.

■■■□ INTERMEDIATE

MATERIALS

Light Weight Yarn

[3] LIGHT

[7 ounces, 575 yards
(198 grams, 525 meters) per skein]:
  Blanket - 4 skeins
  Booties - 60 yards (55 meters)
Crochet hook as indicated below **or**
size needed for gauge
  Blanket
   Size F (3.75 mm)
  Booties
   0 to 3 months - size E (3.5 mm)
   3 to 6 months - size F (3.75 mm)
¹/₄"w (7 mm) Ribbon - 32" (81.5 cm) length

GAUGES
Blanket
In pattern, 18 sc and 19 rows = 4" (10 cm)
Booties
0 to 3 months - 7 dc = 1¹/₂" (3.75 cm)
3 to 6 months - 6 dc = 1¹/₂" (3.75 cm)

GAUGE SWATCHES
Blanket: 4" (10 cm) square
Ch 19.
Work same as Body for 19 rows.
Finish off.

Booties
  0 to 3 months - Approximately 3³/₄" (9.5 cm)
  3 to 6 months - Approximately 4" (10 cm)
Work same as Sole.

STITCH GUIDE

PUFF ST (uses one st)
★ YO, insert hook in st indicated, YO and pull up
a loop even with loop on hook; repeat from ★
2 times **more**, YO and draw through all 7 loops
on hook, ch 1 to close.

BLANKET
Finished Size: 38" x 45¹/₂" (96.5 cm x 115.5 cm)

BODY
Ch 156.

Row 1 (Right side)**:** Sc in back ridge of second ch
from hook *(Fig. 1, page 30)* and each ch across:
155 sc.

Note: Loop a short piece of yarn around any stitch
to mark Row 1 as **right** side.

Row 2: Ch 1, turn; sc in Front Loop Only of each sc
across *(Fig. 3, page 30)*.

Row 3: Ch 1, turn; sc in both loops of each sc
across.

14

Row 4: Ch 1, turn; sc in Front Loop Only of each sc across.

Rows 5-18: Repeat Rows 3 and 4, 7 times.

Row 19: Ch 1, turn; sc in both loops of first 2 sc, ★ work Puff St in free loop of sc one row **below** next sc *(Fig. 2a, page 30)*, skip next sc from last sc worked, sc in both loops of next 2 sc; repeat from ★ across: 104 sc and 51 Puff Sts.

Row 20: Ch 1, turn; skipping ch-1 closings, sc in Front Loop Only of each sc and each Puff St across: 155 sc.

Row 21: Ch 1, turn; sc in both loops of each sc across.

Row 22: Ch 1, turn; sc in Front Loop Only of each sc across.

Row 23: Ch 1, turn; sc in both loops of first 6 sc, work Puff St in free loop of sc one row **below** sc just worked into, skip next sc from last sc worked, sc in both loops of next sc, skip next sc and work Puff St in free loop of sc one row **below** next sc, ★ skip next sc from last sc worked, sc in both loops of next 7 sc, work Puff St in free loop of sc one row **below** next sc, skip next sc from last sc worked, sc in both loops of next sc, work Puff St in free loop of sc one row **below** next sc, skip next sc from last sc worked, sc in both loops of next 7 sc, work Puff St in free loop of sc one row **below** sc just worked into, skip next sc from last sc worked, sc in both loops of next sc, skip next sc and work Puff St in free loop of sc one row **below** next sc; repeat from ★ across to last 7 sc, skip next sc from last sc worked, sc in both loops of last 6 sc: 125 sc and 30 Puff Sts.

Row 24: Ch 1, turn; skipping ch-1 closings, sc in Front Loop Only of each sc and each Puff St across: 155 sc.

Row 25: Ch 1, turn; sc in both loops of first 7 sc, work Puff St in free loop of sc one row **below** next sc, skip next sc from last sc worked, sc in both loops of next 7 sc, ★ work Puff St in free loop of sc one row **below** next sc, skip next sc from last sc worked, sc in both loops of next 3 sc, work Puff St in free loop of sc one row **below** next sc, skip next sc from last sc worked, sc in both loops of next 7 sc, work Puff St in free loop of sc one row **below** next sc, skip next sc from last sc worked, sc in both loops of next 7 sc; repeat from ★ across: 133 sc and 22 Puff Sts.

Row 26: Ch 1, turn; skipping ch-1 closings, sc in Front Loop Only of each sc and each Puff St across: 155 sc.

Row 27: Ch 1, turn; sc in both loops of first 5 sc, skip next sc and work Puff St in free loop of sc one row **below** next sc, skip next sc from last sc worked, sc in both loops of next 3 sc, work Puff St in free loop of sc one row **below** sc just worked into, ★ skip next sc from last sc worked, sc in both loops of next 6 sc, work Puff St in free loop of sc one row **below** next sc, skip next sc from last sc worked, sc in both loops of next sc, work Puff St in free loop of sc one row **below** next sc, skip next sc from last sc worked, sc in both loops of next 6 sc, skip next sc and work Puff St in free loop of sc one row **below** next sc, skip next sc from last sc worked, sc in both loops of next 3 sc, work Puff St in free loop of sc one row **below** sc just worked into; repeat from ★ across to last 6 sc, skip next sc from last sc worked, sc in both loops of last 5 sc: 125 sc and 30 Puff Sts.

Row 28: Ch 1, turn; skipping ch-1 closings, sc in Front Loop Only of each sc and each Puff St across: 155 sc.

Row 29: Ch 1, turn; sc in both loops of each sc across.

Row 30: Ch 1, turn; sc in Front Loop Only of each sc across.

Row 31: Ch 1, turn; sc in both loops of first 2 sc, ★ work Puff St in free loop of sc one row **below** next sc, skip next sc from last sc worked, sc in both loops of next 2 sc; repeat from ★ across: 104 sc and 51 Puff Sts.

Rows 32-198: Repeat Rows 2-31, 5 times; then repeat Rows 2-18 once **more**: 155 sc.

Do **not** finish off.

Instructions continued on page 16.

EDGING

Rnd 1: Ch 1, turn; working in both loops of sts across Row 198, work (Puff St, ch 1) 3 times in first sc, (skip next sc, work Puff St in next sc, ch 1) across to last 2 sc, skip next sc, work (Puff St, ch 1) 3 times in last sc; working in end of rows, skip first 2 rows, (work Puff St in next row, ch 1, skip next row) across; working in free loops of beginning ch **(Fig. 2b, page 30)**, work (Puff St, ch 1) 3 times in first ch, (skip next ch, work Puff St in next ch, ch 1) across to last 2 chs, skip next ch, work (Puff St, ch 1) 3 time in last ch; working in end of rows, skip first row, work Puff St in next row, ch 1, (skip next row, work Puff St in next row, ch 1) across to last 2 rows, skip last 2 rows and join with slip st to top of first Puff St: 360 Puff Sts and 360 sps.

Rnd 2: Ch 1, turn; 2 sc in next sp and in each sp around; join with slip st to first sc: 720 sc.

Rnd 3: Ch 1, turn; work Puff St in same st as joining, ch 1, skip next sc, † work (Puff St, ch 1) 3 times in next sc, skip next sc, (work Puff St in next sc, ch 1, skip next sc) 78 times, work (Puff St, ch 1) 3 times in next sc, skip next sc †, (work Puff St in next sc, ch 1, skip next sc) 100 times, repeat from † to † once, (work Puff St in next sc, ch 1, skip next sc) across; join with slip st to top of first Puff St: 368 Puff Sts and 368 sps.

Rnd 4: Ch 1, turn; 2 sc in next sp and in each sp around; join with slip st to first sc: 736 sc.

Rnd 5: Ch 1, turn; work Puff St in same st as joining, ch 1, skip next sc, work Puff St in next sc, ch 1, skip next sc, † work (Puff St, ch 1) 3 times in next sc, skip next sc, (work Puff St in next sc, ch 1, skip next sc) 80 times, work (Puff St, ch 1) 3 times in next sc, skip next sc †, (work Puff St in next sc, ch 1, skip next sc) 102 times, repeat from † to † once, (work Puff St in next sc, ch 1, skip next sc) across; join with slip st to top of first Puff St: 376 Puff Sts and 376 sps.

Rnd 6: Ch 1, turn; 2 sc in next sp and in each sp around; join with slip st to first sc, finish off.

BOOTIES
SOLE
Ch 13.

Rnd 1 (Right side)**:** 3 Sc in second ch from hook, sc in next 10 chs, 5 sc in last ch; working in free loops of beginning ch **(Fig. 2b, page 30)**, sc in next 10 chs, 2 sc in next ch; join with slip st to Back Loop Only of first sc **(Fig. 3, page 30)**: 30 sc.

Note: Loop a short piece of yarn around any stitch to mark Rnd 1 as **right** side.

Rnd 2: Ch 3 **(counts as first dc, now and throughout unless otherwise indicated)**, working in Back Loops Only, 2 dc in next sc, dc in next 3 sc, hdc in next 4 sc, dc in next 4 sc, 2 dc in each of next 2 sc, dc in next sc, 2 dc in each of next 2 sc, dc in next 4 sc, hdc in next 4 sc, dc in next 3 sc, 2 dc in last sc; join with slip st to first dc, do **not** finish off: 36 sts.

SIDES
Rnd 1: Ch 1, turn; sc in Front Loop Only **(Fig. 3, page 30)** of next st and each st around; join with slip st to **both** loops of first sc.

Rnd 2: Ch 1, turn; ★ sc in both loops of next sc, work Puff St in free loop of st one row **below** next sc, skip next sc from last sc worked, sc in both loops of next 6 sc, work Puff St in free loop of st one row **below** sc just worked into, skip next sc from last sc worked, sc in both loops of next sc, skip next sc and work Puff St in free loop of st one row **below** next sc, skip next sc from last sc worked, sc in both loops of next 6 sc, work Puff St in free loop of st one row **below** next sc, skip next sc from last sc worked; repeat from ★ once **more**; join with slip st to first sc: 28 sc and 8 Puff Sts.

Rnd 3: Ch 1, turn; skipping ch-1 closings, sc in Front Loop Only of next Puff St and each sc and Puff St around; join with slip st to **both** loops of first sc: 36 sc.

Instructions continued on page 18.

To decrease (uses next 2 sts), pull up a loop in each of next 2 sts, YO and draw through all 3 loops on hook **(counts as one sc)**.

Rnd 4: Ch 1, turn; sc in both loops of next 2 sc, work Puff St in free loop of sc one row **below** next sc, skip next sc from last sc worked, sc in both loops of next 6 sc, work Puff St in free loop of sc one row **below** next sc, skip next sc from last sc worked, sc in both loops of next 4 sc, decrease, work Puff St in free loop of sc one row **below** next sc, skip next sc from last sc worked, sc in both loops of next 3 sc, work Puff St in free loop of sc one row **below** next sc, skip next sc from last sc worked, decrease, sc in both loops of next 4 sc, work Puff St in free loop of sc one row **below** next sc, skip next sc from last sc worked, sc in both loops of next 6 sc, work Puff St in free loop of sc one row **below** next sc, skip next sc from last sc worked, sc in both loops of last sc; join with slip st to first sc: 28 sc and 6 Puff Sts.

Rnd 5: Ch 1, turn; working in Front Loops Only and skipping ch-1 closings, sc in next 10 sts, decrease twice, sc in next 5 sts, decrease twice, sc in last 11 sts; join with slip st to both loops of first sc: 30 sc.

Rnd 6: Ch 1, turn; sc in both loops of next sc, work Puff St in free loop of sc one row **below** next sc, skip next sc from last sc worked, sc in both loops of next 5 sc, skip next sc and work Puff St in free loop of sc one row **below** next sc, skip next sc from last sc worked, sc in both loops of next 3 sc, work Puff St in free loop of sc one row **below** sc just worked into, skip next sc from last sc worked, sc in both loops of next 2 sc, work Puff St in free loop of sc one row **below** next sc, skip next sc from last sc worked, sc in both loops of next sc, work Puff St in free loop of sc one row **below** next sc, skip next sc from last sc worked, sc in both loops of next 2 sc, skip next sc and work Puff St in free loop of sc one row **below** next sc, skip next sc from last sc worked, sc in both loops of next 3 sc, work Puff St in free loop of sc one row **below** sc just worked into, skip next sc from last sc worked, sc in both loops of next 5 sc, work Puff St in free loop of sc one row **below** last sc, skip last sc; join with slip st to top of first sc: 22 sc and 8 Puff Sts.

Rnd 7: Ch 1, turn; working in Front Loops Only and skipping ch-1 closings, sc in next 11 sts, decrease, sc in next 3 sts, decrease, sc in last 12 sts; join with slip st to both loops of first sc: 28 sc.

CUFF

Rnd 1 (Eyelet rnd)**:** Ch 3 **(counts as first hdc plus ch 1)**, turn; working in both loops, skip next sc, (hdc in next sc, ch 1, skip next sc) 5 times, (dc in next sc, ch 1, skip next sc) 4 times, (hdc in next sc, ch 1, skip next sc) 4 times; join with slip st to first hdc: 14 ch-1 sps.

Rnd 2: Ch 1, do **not** turn; 2 sc in next ch-1 sp and in each ch-1 sp around; join with slip st to first sc: 28 sc.

Rnd 3: Ch 1, turn; sc in Front Loop Only of next sc and each sc around; join with slip st to **both** loops of first sc.

Rnd 4: Ch 1, turn; sc in both loops of next sc and each sc around; join with slip st to first sc.

Rnd 5: Ch 1, do **not** turn; work Puff St in same st as joining, ch 1, skip next sc, ★ work Puff St in next sc, ch 1, skip next sc; repeat from ★ around; join with slip st to top of first Puff St: 14 sps.

Rnd 6: Ch 1, turn; 2 sc in next sp and in each sp around; join with slip st to first sc, finish off.

Beginning at center front, weave a 16" (40.5 cm) length of ribbon through Eyelet rnd.

Buds & Blooms

Shown on page 21.

⬤⬤⬤◻ **INTERMEDIATE**

MATERIALS

Light Weight Yarn 🧶**3** **LIGHT**
[1.75 ounces, 161 yards
(50 grams, 147 meters) per skein]:
Blanket
White - 7 skeins
Yellow - 4 skeins
Booties
White - 45 yards (41 meters)
Yellow - 45 yards (41 meters)
Crochet hook as indicated below **or**
size needed for gauge
Blanket
Size F (3.75 mm)
Booties
0 to 3 months - size E (3.5 mm)
3 to 6 months - size F (3.75 mm)
$1/4$"w (7 mm) Ribbon - 32" (81.5 cm) length
Safety pins - 2
Yarn needle

GAUGES
Blanket
One Square = $5^1/_2$" (14 cm)
In pattern, 17 sts [sc, (ch 1, sc) 8 times] = 4" (10 cm)
Booties
0 to 3 months - 7 dc = $1^1/_2$" (3.75 cm)
3 to 6 months - 6 dc = $1^1/_2$" (3.75 cm)

GAUGE SWATCHES
Blanket: $3^1/_4$" (8.25 cm) square
Work same as Square through Rnd 4.

Booties
0 to 3 months - Approximately $3^3/_4$" (9.5 cm)
3 to 6 months - Approximately 4" (10 cm)
Work same as Sole.

STITCH GUIDE

POPCORN (uses one st or sp)
3 Sc in st or sp indicated, drop loop from hook, insert hook from **front** to **back** in first sc of 3-sc group, hook dropped loop and draw through st.

BLANKET
Finished Size: $38^1/_2$" (98 cm) square

SQUARE (Make 36)
With Yellow, ch 4; join with slip st to form a ring.

Rnd 1 (Right side)**:** Ch 1, (sc in ring, ch 3) 4 times; join with slip st to first sc: 4 sc and 4 ch-3 sps.

Note: Loop a short piece of yarn around any stitch to mark Rnd 1 as **right** side.

Rnd 2: ★ (Slip st, ch 2, 3 dc, ch 2, slip st) in next ch-3 sp, ch 3; repeat from ★ around; join with slip st to first slip st, finish off: 4 Petals and 4 ch-3 sps.

Instructions continued on page 20.

Rnd 3: With **right** side facing, join White with slip st in any ch-3 sp between Petals; ch 4 **(counts as first dc plus ch 1, now and throughout)**, (dc, ch 1, dc) in same sp, ch 2, ★ keeping next Petal toward you, dc in next ch-3 sp between Petals, (ch 1, dc in same sp) 3 times, ch 2; repeat from ★ 2 times **more**, keeping next Petal toward you, dc in same sp as joining slip st, ch 1; join with slip st to first dc: 16 dc and 16 sps.

Rnd 4: Slip st in next corner ch-1 sp, ch 4, (dc, ch 1) twice in same sp, (dc in next sp, ch 1) 3 times, ★ (dc, ch 1) 4 times in next corner ch-1 sp, (dc in next sp, ch 1) 3 times; repeat from ★ 2 times **more**, dc in same corner ch-1 sp as first slip st, ch 1; join with slip st to first dc, place loop from hook onto safety pin to keep piece from unraveling as you work the next rnd: 28 dc and 28 ch-1 sps.

Keep safety pin with loop and working yarn on wrong side of work throughout.

Rnd 5: With **right** side facing, join Yellow with slip st in first corner ch-1 sp; ch 1, work (Popcorn, ch 3, Popcorn) in same sp, ch 1, (sc in next ch-1 sp, ch 1) twice, (work Popcorn in next ch-1 sp, ch 1) twice, (sc in next ch-1 sp, ch 1) twice, ★ work (Popcorn, ch 3, Popcorn) in next corner ch-1 sp, ch 1, (sc in next ch-1 sp, ch 1) twice, (work Popcorn in next ch-1 sp, ch 1) twice, (sc in next ch-1 sp, ch 1) twice; repeat from ★ 2 times **more**; join with slip st to top of first Popcorn, place loop from hook onto second safety pin to keep piece from unraveling as you work the next rnd: 16 Popcorns and 32 sps.

Rnd 6: With **right** side facing, remove first safety pin and, with hook **behind** sts of Rnd 5, place loop onto hook; ch 2, (sc, ch 1) twice in first corner ch-3 sp, (sc in next ch-1 sp, ch 1) 7 times, ★ (sc, ch 1) twice in next corner ch-1 sp, (sc in next ch-1 sp, ch 1) 7 times; repeat from ★ 2 times **more**; join with slip st to first sc, place loop from hook onto first safety pin to keep piece from unraveling as you work the next rnd: 36 ch-1 sps.

Rnd 7: With **right** side facing, remove second safety pin and, with hook **behind** sts of Rnd 6, place loop onto hook; ch 2, work (Popcorn, ch 3, Popcorn) in first corner ch-1 sp, (ch 1, sc in next ch-1 sp) 3 times, ch 2, skip next ch-1 sp, work Popcorn in next sc, ch 2, skip next ch-1 sp, (sc in next ch-1 sp, ch 1) 3 times, ★ work (Popcorn, ch 3, Popcorn) in next corner ch-1 sp, (ch 1, sc in next ch-1 sp) 3 times, ch 2, skip next ch-1 sp, work Popcorn in next sc, ch 2, skip next ch-1 sp, (sc in next ch-1 sp, ch 1) 3 times; repeat from ★ 2 times **more**; join with slip st to top of first Popcorn, finish off: 12 Popcorns and 36 sps.

Rnd 8: With **right** side facing, remove first safety pin and, with hook **behind** sts of Rnd 7, place loop onto hook; ch 2, (sc, ch 1) twice in first corner ch-3 sp, (sc in next sp, ch 1) 8 times, ★ (sc, ch 1) twice in next corner ch-1 sp, (sc in next sp, ch 1) 8 times; repeat from ★ 2 times **more**; join with slip st to first sc, do **not** finish off: 40 ch-1 sps.

Rnd 9: Slip st in next corner ch-1 sp, ch 1, (sc in same sp, ch 1) twice, (sc in next ch-1 sp, ch 1) 9 times, ★ (sc, ch 1) twice in next ch-1 sp, (sc in next ch-1 sp, ch 1) 9 times; repeat from ★ 2 times **more**; join with slip st to first sc, finish off: 44 ch-1 sps.

ASSEMBLY
Join Squares as follows:
With **right** side of **first Square** facing, join White with slip st in any corner ch-1 sp; ch 1, holding **second Square** with **wrong** side facing, slip st in corresponding corner ch-1 sp, ch 1, ★ slip st in next ch-1 sp on **first Square**, ch 1, slip st in next ch-1 sp on **second Square**, ch 1; repeat from ★ across to next corner ch-1 sp on **first Square**, slip st in corner ch-1 sp on **first Square**, ch 1, slip st in next corner ch-1 sp on **second Square**, ch 1, slip st in same corner sp on **first Square**; finish off.

Join Squares together forming 6 vertical strips of 6 Squares each; then join strips together in same manner.

Instructions continued on page 22.

EDGING

Rnd 1: With **right** side facing, join White with slip st in any corner ch-1 sp; ch 1, (sc in same sp, ch 1) twice, ★ (sc in next sp, ch 1) across to next corner ch-1 sp, (sc, ch 1) twice in corner ch-1 sp; repeat from ★ 2 times **more**, (sc in next sp, ch 1) across; join with slip st to first sc.

Rnd 2: Slip st in next corner ch-1 sp, ch 1, (sc in same sp, ch 1) twice, ★ (sc in next ch-1 sp, ch 1) across to next corner ch-1 sp, (sc, ch 1) twice in corner ch-1 sp; repeat from ★ 2 times **more**, (sc in next sp, ch 1) across; join with slip st to first sc, finish off.

Rnd 3: With **right** side facing, join Yellow with slip st in any corner ch-1 sp; ch 1, work (Popcorn, ch 3, Popcorn) in same sp, ch 1, ★ (sc in next ch-1 sp, ch 1) across to next corner ch-1 sp, work (Popcorn, ch 3, Popcorn) in corner ch-1 sp, ch 1; repeat from ★ 2 times **more**, (sc in next ch-1 sp, ch 1) across; join with slip st to top of first Popcorn, finish off.

Rnd 4: With **right** side facing, join White with slip st in any corner ch-3 sp; ch 1, (sc in same sp, ch 1) twice, ★ (sc in next ch-1 sp, ch 1) across to next corner ch-3 sp, (sc, ch 1) twice in corner ch-3 sp; repeat from ★ 2 times **more**, (sc in next ch-1 sp, ch 1) across; join with slip st to first sc, do **not** finish off.

Rnd 5: Slip st in next corner ch-1 sp, ch 1, (sc in same sp, ch 1) twice, ★ (sc in next ch-1 sp, ch 1) across to next corner ch-1 sp, (sc, ch 1) twice in corner ch-1 sp; repeat from ★ 2 times **more**, (sc in next ch-1 sp, ch 1) across; join with slip st to first sc, finish off.

Rnd 6: With **right** side facing, join Yellow with slip st in any corner ch-1 sp; ch 1, work (Popcorn, ch 3, Popcorn) in same sp, ch 1, ★ (sc in next ch-1 sp, ch 1) across to next corner ch-1 sp, work (Popcorn, ch 3, Popcorn) in corner ch-1 sp, ch 1; repeat from ★ 2 times **more**, (sc in next ch-1 sp, ch 1) across; join with slip st to top of first Popcorn, finish off.

Rnd 7: With **right** side facing, join White with slip st in any corner ch-3 sp; ch 1, (sc in same sp, ch 1) twice, ★ (sc in next ch-1 sp, ch 1) across to next corner ch-3 sp, (sc, ch 1) twice in corner ch-3 sp; repeat from ★ 2 times **more**, (sc in next ch-1 sp, ch 1) across; join with slip st to first sc, do **not** finish off.

Rnd 8: Slip st in next corner ch-1 sp, ch 1, (sc in same sp, ch 1) twice, ★ (sc in next ch-1 sp, ch 1) across to next corner ch-1 sp, (sc, ch 1) twice in corner ch-1 sp; repeat from ★ 2 times **more**, (sc in next ch-1 sp, ch 1) across; join with slip st to first sc.

Rnd 9: ★ Slip st in next ch-1 sp, ch 2, slip st in back ridge of second ch from hook *(Fig. 1, page 30)*; repeat from ★ around; join with slip st to first slip st, finish off.

BOOTIES
SOLE
With Yellow, ch 13.

Rnd 1 (Right side)**:** 3 Sc in second ch from hook, sc in next 10 chs, 5 sc in last ch; working in free loops of beginning ch *(Fig. 2b, page 30)*, sc in next 10 chs, 2 sc in next ch; join with slip st to Back Loop Only of first sc *(Fig. 3, page 30)*: 30 sc.

Note: Loop a short piece of yarn around any stitch to mark Rnd 1 as **right** side.

Rnd 2: Ch 3 **(counts as first dc, now and throughout unless otherwise indicated)**, working in Back Loops Only, 2 dc in next sc, dc in next 3 sc, hdc in next 4 sc, dc in next 4 sc, 2 dc in each of next 2 sc, dc in next sc, 2 dc in each of next 2 sc, dc in next 4 sc, hdc in next 4 sc, dc in next 3 sc, 2 dc in next sc; join with slip st to first dc, finish off: 36 sts.

SIDES

Rnd 1: With **right** side facing and working in Back Loops Only, join White with sc in same st as joining *(see Joining With Sc, page 30)*; sc in next st and in each st around; join with slip st to **both** loops of first sc.

Rnd 2: Ch 1, sc in same st as joining, ch 1, skip next sc, ★ sc in next sc, ch 1, skip next sc; repeat from ★ around; join with slip st to first sc: 18 ch-1 sps.

Rnd 3: Slip st in next ch-1 sp changing to Yellow, do **not** cut White; ch 1, sc in same sp, ch 1, (sc in next ch-1 sp, ch 1) around; join with slip st to first sc changing to White, cut Yellow.

Rnds 4 and 5: (Slip st, ch 1, sc) in next ch-1 sp, ch 1, (sc in next ch-1 sp, ch 1) around; join with slip st to first sc, do **not** finish off.

Rnd 6: Slip st in next ch-1 sp changing to Yellow, do **not** cut White; ch 1, sc in same sp, ch 1, (sc in next ch-1 sp, ch 1) 3 times, dc in each of next 7 ch-1 sps, ch 1, (sc in next ch-1 sp, ch 1) 7 times; join with slip st to first sc: 18 sts and 12 ch-1 sps.

Rnd 7: Slip st in next ch-1 sp changing to White, cut Yellow; ch 1, sc in same sp, ch 1, (sc in next ch-1 sp, ch 1) 3 times, skip next dc, (sc in next dc, ch 1, skip next dc) 3 times, (sc in next ch-1 sp, ch 1) 8 times; join with slip st to first sc, do **not** finish off: 15 ch-1 sps.

CUFF

Rnd 1 (Eyelet rnd): Slip st in next ch-1 sp, ch 3 **(counts as first hdc plus ch 1)**, (hdc in next ch-1 sp, ch 1) around; join with slip st to first hdc.

Rnd 2: (Slip st, ch 1, sc) in next ch-1 sp, ch 1, (sc in next ch-1 sp, ch 1) around; join with slip st to first sc, finish off.

Rnd 3: With **right** side facing, join Yellow with sc in fourth ch-1 sp **before** joining; ch 1, sc in next ch-1 sp, ch 1, (work Popcorn in next ch-1 sp, ch 1) twice, ★ (sc in next ch-1 sp, ch 1) 3 times, (work Popcorn in next ch-1 sp, ch 1) twice; repeat from ★ once **more**, sc in last ch-1 sp, ch 1; join with slip st to first sc, do **not** finish off: 9 sc, 6 Popcorns, and 15 ch-1 sps.

Rnd 4: Slip st in next ch-1 sp changing to White, do **not** cut Yellow; ch 1, sc in same sp, ch 1, (sc in next ch-1 sp, ch 1) around; join with slip st to first sc, do **not** finish off.

Rnd 5: Slip st in next ch-1 sp changing to Yellow, do **not** cut White; ch 1, sc in same sp, ch 2, skip next ch-1 sp, work Popcorn in next sc, ch 2, skip next ch-1 sp, ★ sc in next ch-1 sp, (ch 1, sc in next ch-1 sp) twice, ch 2, skip next ch-1 sp, work Popcorn in next sc, ch 2, skip next ch-1 sp; repeat from ★ once **more**, (sc in next ch-1 sp, ch 1) twice; join with slip st to first sc: 12 sps.

Rnd 6: Slip st in next ch-1 sp changing to White, cut Yellow; ch 1, sc in same sp, ch 1, (sc in next sp, ch 1) around; join with slip st to first sc, do **not** finish off.

Rnd 7: (Slip st, ch 1, sc) in next ch-1 sp, ch 1, (sc in next ch-1 sp, ch 1) around; join with slip st to first sc.

Rnd 8: ★ Slip st in next ch-1 sp, ch 2, slip st in back ridge of second ch from hook *(Fig. 1, page 30)*; repeat from ★ around; join with slip st to first slip st, finish off.

Beginning at center front, weave a 16" (40.5 cm) length of ribbon through Eyelet rnd.

FLOWER

With Yellow, ch 4; join with slip st to form a ring.

Rnd 1 (Right side): (Sc in ring, ch 3) 4 times; join with slip st to first sc: 4 ch-3 sps.

Rnd 2: (Slip st, ch 2, 3 dc, ch 2, slip st) in each ch-3 sp around; join with slip st to first slip st, finish off leaving a long end for sewing.

Sew Flower to top of Bootie (below Tie).

Precious in Pink

Shown on page 27.

■■■□ INTERMEDIATE

MATERIALS

Light Weight Yarn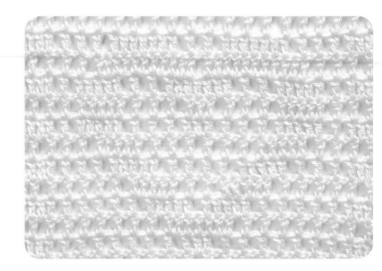
[5 ounces, 468 yards
(140 grams, 429 meters) per skein]:
  Blanket - 3 skeins
  Booties - 65 yards (59 meters)
Crochet hook as indicated below **or**
size needed for gauge
  Blanket
    Size F (3.75 mm)
  Booties
    0 to 3 months - size E (3.5 mm)
    3 to 6 months - size F (3.75 mm)
$^1/_4$"w (7 mm) Ribbon - 32" (81.5 cm) length
Yarn needle

GAUGES

Blanket
In pattern, 16 sts and 8 rows = 4" (10 cm)
One Panel = $10^1/_4$" (26 cm) wide
Booties
0 to 3 months - 7 dc = $1^1/_2$" (3.75 cm)
3 to 6 months - 6 dc = $1^1/_2$" (3.75 cm)

GAUGE SWATCHES

Blanket: 4" (10 cm) square
Ch 18.
Row 1: Dc in fourth ch from hook **(3 skipped chs count as first dc)** and in each ch across: 16 dc.
Rows 2-8: Ch 3 **(counts as first dc)**, turn; dc in next dc and in each dc across.
Finish off.

Booties
  0 to 3 months - Approximately $3^3/_4$" (9.5 cm)
  3 to 6 months - Approximately 4" (10 cm)
Work same as Sole.

BLANKET

Finished Size: 35" x $45^1/_2$" (89 cm x 115.5 cm)

PANEL (Make 3)

Ch 43, place a marker in third ch from hook for st placement.

Row 1 (Right side)**:** Dc in fourth ch from hook **(3 skipped chs count as first dc)** and in next 2 chs, ch 1, ★ skip next ch, dc in next 3 chs, ch 1; repeat from ★ across to last 5 chs, skip next ch, dc in last 4 chs: 32 dc and 9 ch-1 sps.

Note: Loop a short piece of yarn around any stitch to mark Row 1 as **right** side and bottom edge.

Row 2: Ch 3 **(counts as first dc, now and throughout)**, turn; dc in next dc, ch 1, ★ skip next dc, dc in next dc and in next ch-1 sp, dc in next dc, ch 1; repeat from ★ across to last 3 dc, skip next dc, dc in last 2 dc: 31 dc and 10 ch-1 sps.

Row 3: Ch 3, turn; dc in next dc and in next ch-1 sp, ★ dc in next dc, ch 1, skip next dc, dc in next dc and in next ch-1 sp; repeat from ★ across to last 2 dc, dc in last 2 dc: 32 dc and 9 ch-1 sps.

Row 4: Ch 3, turn; dc in next dc, ch 1, ★ skip next dc, (dc in next dc, ch 1) twice; repeat from ★ across to last 3 dc, skip next dc, dc in last 2 dc: 22 dc and 19 ch-1 sps.

Row 5: Ch 3, turn; dc in next dc and in next ch-1 sp, dc in next dc, (ch 1, dc in next dc) across to last ch-1 sp, dc in last ch-1 sp and in last 2 dc: 24 dc and 17 ch-1 sps.

Row 6: Ch 3, turn; dc in next dc, ch 1, skip next dc, (dc in next dc, ch 1) across to last 3 dc, skip next dc, dc in last 2 dc: 22 dc and 19 ch-1 sps.

Row 7: Ch 3, turn; dc in next dc and in next ch-1 sp, ★ (dc in next dc, ch 1) 8 times, dc in next dc and in next ch-1 sp; repeat from ★ once **more**, dc in last 2 dc: 25 dc and 16 ch-1 sps.

Row 8: Ch 3, turn; dc in next dc, ch 1, skip next dc, (dc in next dc, ch 1) 7 times, dc in next dc and in next ch-1 sp, dc in next 3 dc and in next ch-1 sp, (dc in next dc, ch 1) 8 times, skip next dc, dc in last 2 dc.

Row 9: Ch 3, turn; dc in next dc and in next ch-1 sp, (dc in next dc, ch 1) 6 times, dc in next dc and in next ch-1 sp, dc in next 3 dc, ch 1, skip next dc, dc in next 3 dc and in next ch-1 sp, (dc in next dc, ch 1) 6 times, dc in next dc and in next ch-1 sp, dc in last 2 dc: 28 dc and 13 ch-1 sps.

Row 10: Ch 3, turn; dc in next dc, ch 1, skip next dc, (dc in next dc, ch 1) 5 times, dc in next dc and in next ch-1 sp, dc in next 3 dc, ch 1, skip next dc, (dc in next dc, ch 1) twice, skip next dc, dc in next 3 dc and in next ch-1 sp, (dc in next dc, ch 1) 6 times, skip next dc, dc in last 2 dc: 26 dc and 15 ch-1 sps.

Row 11: Ch 3, turn; dc in next dc and in next ch-1 sp, (dc in next dc, ch 1) 4 times, dc in next dc and in next ch-1 sp, dc in next 3 dc, ch 1, skip next dc, (dc in next dc, ch 1) 4 times, skip next dc, dc in next 3 dc and in next ch-1 sp, (dc in next dc, ch 1) 4 times, dc in next dc and in next ch-1 sp, dc in last 2 dc: 28 dc and 13 ch-1 sps.

Row 12: Ch 3, turn; dc in next dc, ch 1, skip next dc, (dc in next dc, ch 1) 3 times, dc in next dc and in next ch-1 sp, dc in next 3 dc, ch 1, skip next dc, (dc in next dc, ch 1) 6 times, skip next dc, dc in next 3 dc and in next ch-1 sp, (dc in next dc, ch 1) 4 times, skip next dc, dc in last 2 dc: 26 dc and 15 ch-1 sps.

Row 13: Ch 3, turn; dc in next dc and in next ch-1 sp, (dc in next dc, ch 1) twice, dc in next dc and in next ch-1 sp, dc in next 3 dc, ch 1, skip next dc, (dc in next dc, ch 1) 3 times, dc in next dc and in next ch-1 sp, (dc in next dc, ch 1) 4 times, skip next dc, dc in next 3 dc and in next ch-1 sp, (dc in next dc, ch 1) twice, dc in next dc and in next ch-1 sp, dc in last 2 dc: 29 dc and 12 ch-1 sps.

Row 14: Ch 3, turn; dc in next dc, ch 1, skip next dc, (dc in next dc, ch 1) twice, dc in next 5 dc, ch 1, (dc in next dc, ch 1) 3 times, dc in next 3 dc, ch 1, (dc in next dc, ch 1) 3 times, dc in next 5 dc, ch 1, (dc in next dc, ch 1) twice, skip next dc, dc in last 2 dc: 27 dc and 14 ch-1 sps.

Row 15: Ch 3, turn; dc in next dc and in next ch-1 sp, (dc in next dc, ch 1) twice, dc in next 5 dc, ch 1, (dc in next dc, ch 1) twice, dc in next dc and in next ch-1 sp, dc in next 3 dc and in next ch-1 sp, (dc in next dc, ch 1) 3 times, dc in next 5 dc, ch 1, dc in next dc, ch 1, dc in next dc and in next ch-1 sp, dc in last 2 dc: 31 dc and 10 ch-1 sps.

Row 16: Ch 3, turn; dc in next dc, ch 1, skip next dc, (dc in next dc, ch 1) 3 times, skip next dc, ★ dc in next 3 dc and in next ch-1 sp, (dc in next dc and in next ch-1 sp) twice, dc in next 3 dc, ch 1, skip next dc; repeat from ★ once **more**, (dc in next dc, ch 1) 3 times, skip next dc, dc in last 2 dc: 32 dc and 9 ch-1 sps.

Row 17: Ch 3, turn; dc in next dc and in next ch-1 sp, (dc in next dc, ch 1) 4 times, skip next dc, dc in next 7 dc, ch 1, skip next dc, (dc in next dc, ch 1) twice, skip next dc, dc in next 7 dc, ch 1, skip next dc, (dc in next dc, ch 1) 3 times, dc in next dc and in next ch-1 sp, dc in last 2 dc: 30 dc and 11 ch-1 sps.

Instructions continued on page 26.

Row 18: Ch 3, turn; dc in next dc, ch 1, skip next dc, (dc in next dc, ch 1) 5 times, skip next dc, (dc in next dc, ch 1, skip next dc) twice, (dc in next dc, ch 1) 4 times, skip next dc, (dc in next dc, ch 1, skip next dc) twice, (dc in next dc, ch 1) 5 times, skip next dc, dc in last 2 dc: 22 dc and 19 ch-1 sps.

Row 19: Ch 3, turn; dc in next dc and in next ch-1 sp, dc in next dc, (ch 1, dc in next dc) across to last ch-1 sp, dc in last ch-1 sp and in last 2 dc: 24 dc and 17 ch-1 sps.

Row 20: Ch 3, turn; dc in next dc, ch 1, skip next dc, (dc in next dc, ch 1) across to last 3 dc, skip next dc, dc in last 2 dc: 22 dc and 19 ch-1 sps.

Row 21: Ch 3, turn; dc in next dc and in next ch-1 sp, ★ dc in next dc, ch 1, dc in next dc and in next ch-1 sp; repeat from ★ across to last 2 dc, dc in last 2 dc: 32 dc and 9 ch-1 sps.

Rows 22-83: Repeat Rows 2-21, 3 times; then repeat Rows 2 and 3 once **more**; do **not** finish off.

BORDER

With **right** side facing and working in end of rows, (slip st, ch 3, dc) in Row 83, 2 dc in next row and in each row across; working in free loops of beginning ch *(Fig. 2b, page 30)*, (2 dc, ch 2, 2 dc) in first ch, dc in each ch across to marked ch, (2 dc, ch 2, 2 dc) in marked ch; working in end of rows, 2 dc in each row across; (2 dc, ch 2, 2 dc) in first dc on Row 83, dc in each dc and in each ch across to last dc, (2 dc, ch 2, 2 dc) in last dc; join with slip st to first dc, finish off: 426 dc and 4 ch-2 sps.

ASSEMBLY

Join Panels as follows:
Place two Panels with **wrong** sides of long edge together and bottom edges at the same end. Sew through second ch on first corner of both pieces once to secure the beginning of the seam, leaving an ample yarn end to weave in later. Working through **inside** loops of each stitch of **both** pieces, insert the needle from **front** to **back** through first stitch and pull yarn through *(Fig. A)*, ★ insert the needle from **front** to **back** through next stitch and pull yarn through; repeat from ★ across ending in first ch of next corner.

EDGING

Rnd 1: With **right** side of short edge facing, join yarn with slip st in first corner ch-2 sp; ch 5 **(counts as first dc plus ch 2)**, 2 dc in same corner sp, † ch 1, (skip next dc, dc in next 3 dc, ch 1) 10 times, skip next dc, dc in next 2 dc and in next ch, ch 1, skip next joining and next ch, dc in next 3 dc, ch 1, (skip next dc, dc in next 3 dc, ch 1) 10 times, skip next ch and next joining, dc in next ch and in next 2 dc, ch 1, skip next dc, (dc in next 3 dc, ch 1, skip next dc) 10 times, (2 dc, ch 2, 2 dc) in next corner ch-2 sp †, (ch 1, skip next dc, dc in next 3 dc) across to within 2 dc of next corner ch-2 sp, ch 1, skip next 2 dc, (2 dc, ch 2, 2 dc) in corner ch-2 sp, repeat from † to † once, ch 1, skip next 2 dc, (dc in next 3 dc, ch 1, skip next dc) across, dc in same corner sp as joining; join with slip st to first dc: 466 dc and 4 ch-2 sps.

Rnds 2 and 3: (Slip st, ch 5, 2 dc) in next corner sp, ★ † ch 1, skip next dc, (dc in next dc and in next ch-1 sp, dc in next dc, ch 1, skip next dc) across to next corner ch-2 sp †, (2 dc, ch 2, 2 dc) in corner sp; repeat from ★ 2 times **more**, then repeat from † to † once, dc in same corner sp as first dc; join with slip st to first dc.

Finish off.

Fig. A

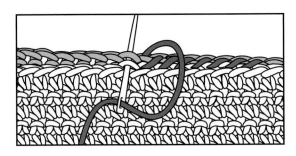

Instructions continued on page 28.

BOOTIES
SOLE
Ch 13.

Rnd 1 (Right side): 3 Sc in second ch from hook, sc in next 10 chs, 5 sc in last ch; working in free loops of beginning ch **(Fig. 2b, page 30)**, sc in next 10 chs, 2 sc in next ch; join with slip st to Back Loop Only of first sc **(Fig. 3, page 30)**: 30 sc.

Note: Loop a short piece of yarn around any stitch to mark Rnd 1 as **right** side.

Rnd 2: Ch 3 **(counts as first dc, now and throughout unless otherwise indicated)**, working in Back Loops Only, 2 dc in next sc, dc in next 3 sc, hdc in next 4 sc, dc in next 4 sc, 2 dc in each of next 2 sc, dc in next sc, 2 dc in each of next 2 sc, dc in next 4 sc, hdc in next 4 sc, dc in next 3 sc, 2 dc in last sc; join with slip st to first dc, do **not** finish off: 36 sts.

SIDES
Rnd 1: Ch 3, dc in Back Loop Only of next st and each st around; join with slip st to first dc.

Rnd 2: Ch 3, dc in both loops of next dc and each dc around; join with slip st to first dc.

To decrease (uses next 2 sts), ★ YO, insert hook in **next** st, YO and pull up a loop, YO and draw through 2 loops on hook; repeat from ★ once **more**, YO and draw through all 3 loops on hook **(counts as one dc)**.

Rnd 3: Ch 1, sc in same st as joining and in next 11 dc, decrease, (dc in next dc, decrease) 3 times, sc in last 13 dc; join with slip st to first sc: 32 sts.

Rnd 4: Ch 1, sc in same st as joining and in next 11 sc, decrease 4 times, sc in last 12 sc; join with slip st to first sc: 28 sts.

CUFF
Rnd 1 (Eyelet rnd): Ch 3 **(counts as first hdc plus ch 1)**, skip next st, (hdc in next st, ch 1, skip next st) 4 times, (dc in next st, ch 1, skip next st) 5 times, (hdc in next st, ch 1, skip next st) 4 times; join with slip st to first hdc: 14 ch-1 sps.

Rnd 2: Ch 1, 2 sc in each ch-1 sp around; join with slip st to first sc: 28 sc.

Rnd 3: Ch 4 **(counts as first dc plus ch 1, now and throughout)**, ★ skip next sc, dc in next 3 sc, ch 1; repeat from ★ around to last 3 sc, skip next sc, dc in last 2 sc; join with slip st to first dc: 21 dc and 7 ch-1 sps.

Rnd 4: Ch 3, dc in next ch-1 sp and in next dc, ch 1, skip next dc, ★ dc in next dc and in next ch-1 sp, dc in next dc, ch 1, skip next dc; repeat from ★ around; join with slip st to first dc.

Rnd 5: Ch 4, skip next dc, dc in next dc and in next ch-1 sp, ★ dc in next dc, ch 1, skip next dc, dc in next dc and in next ch-1 sp; repeat from ★ around; join with slip st to first dc, finish off.

Beginning at center front, weave a 16" (40.5 cm) length of ribbon through Eyelet rnd.

General Instructions

ABBREVIATIONS

BPdc	Back Post double crochet(s)
ch(s)	chain(s)
cm	centimeters
dc	double crochet(s)
FP	Front Post
FPdc	Front Post double crochet(s)
hdc	half double crochet(s)
mm	millimeters
Rnd(s)	Round(s)
sc	single crochet(s)
sp(s)	space(s)
st(s)	stitch(es)
YO	yarn over

★ — work instructions following ★ as many **more** times as indicated in addition to the first time.

† to † — work all instructions from first † to second † **as many** times as specified.

( ) or [ ] — work enclosed instructions **as many** times as specified by the number immediately following **or** work all enclosed instructions in the stitch or space indicated **or** contains explanatory remarks.

colon (:) — the number(s) given after a colon at the end of a row or round denote(s) the number of stitches you should have on that row or round.

CROCHET TERMINOLOGY

UNITED STATES		INTERNATIONAL
slip stitch (slip st)	=	single crochet (sc)
single crochet (sc)	=	double crochet (dc)
half double crochet (hdc)	=	half treble crochet (htr)
double crochet (dc)	=	treble crochet(tr)
treble crochet (tr)	=	double treble crochet (dtr)
double treble crochet (dtr)	=	triple treble crochet (ttr)
triple treble crochet (tr tr)	=	quadruple treble crochet (qtr)
skip	=	miss

Yarn Weight Symbol & Names	LACE 0	SUPER FINE 1	FINE 2	LIGHT 3	MEDIUM 4	BULKY 5	SUPER BULKY 6
Type of Yarns in Category	Fingering, 10-count crochet thread	Sock, Fingering Baby	Sport, Baby	DK, Light Worsted	Worsted, Afghan, Aran	Chunky, Craft, Rug	Bulky, Roving
Crochet Gauge* Ranges in Single Crochet to 4" (10 cm)	32-42 double crochets**	21-32 sts	16-20 sts	12-17 sts	11-14 sts	8-11 sts	5-9 sts
Advised Hook Size Range	Steel*** 6,7,8 Regular hook B-1	B-1 to E-4	E-4 to 7	7 to I-9	I-9 to K-10.5	K-10.5 to M-13	M-13 and larger

*GUIDELINES ONLY: The chart above reflects the most commonly used gauges and hook sizes for specific yarn categories.

** Lace weight yarns are usually crocheted on larger-size hooks to create lacy openwork patterns. Accordingly, a gauge range is difficult to determine. Always follow the gauge stated in your pattern.

*** Steel crochet hooks are sized differently from regular hooks–the higher the number the smaller the hook, which is the reverse of regular hook sizing.

CROCHET HOOKS													
U.S.	B-1	C-2	D-3	E-4	F-5	G-6	H-8	I-9	J-10	K-10½	N	P	Q
Metric - mm	2.25	2.75	3.25	3.5	3.75	4	5	5.5	6	6.5	9	10	15

■□□□ BEGINNER	Projects for first-time crocheters using basic stitches. Minimal shaping.
■■□□ EASY	Projects using yarn with basic stitches, repetitive stitch patterns, simple color changes, and simple shaping and finishing.
■■■□ INTERMEDIATE	Projects using a variety of techniques, such as basic lace patterns or color patterns, mid-level shaping and finishing.
■■■■ EXPERIENCED	Projects with intricate stitch patterns, techniques and dimension, such as non-repeating patterns, multi-color techniques, fine threads, small hooks, detailed shaping and refined finishing.

GAUGE

Exact gauge is **essential** for proper size and fit. Before beginning your project, make the sample swatch given in the individual instructions in the yarn and hook specified. After completing the swatch, measure it, counting your stitches and rows or rounds carefully. If your swatch is larger or smaller than specified, **make another, changing hook size to get the correct gauge**. Keep trying until you find the size hook that will give you the specified gauge.

HINTS

As in all crochet pieces, good finishing techniques make a big difference in the quality of the piece. Make a habit of taking care of loose ends as you work. To keep loose ends from showing, always weave them back through several stitches or work over them. When ends are secure, clip them off close to the work.

JOINING WITH SC

When instructed to join with a sc, begin with a slip knot on the hook. Insert the hook in the stitch or space indicated, YO and pull up a loop, YO and draw through both loops on hook.

BACK RIDGE OF A CHAIN

Work only in the loops indicated by arrows *(Fig. 1)*.

Fig. 1

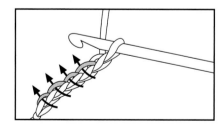

FREE LOOPS

After working in Back or Front Loops Only on a row or round, there will be a ridge of unused loops. These are called the free loops. Later, when instructed to work in free loops of the same row or round, work in these loops *(Fig. 2a)*.
When instructed to work in the free loops of a chain, work in the loop indicated by the arrow *(Fig. 2b)*.

Fig. 2a   Fig. 2b

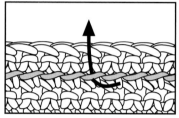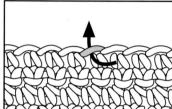

FRONT OR BACK LOOP ONLY

Work only in the loop(s) indicated by the arrow *(Fig. 3)*.

Fig. 3

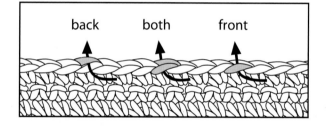

POST STITCH

Work around the post of the stitch indicated, inserting the hook in the direction of the arrow *(Fig. 4)*.

Fig. 4

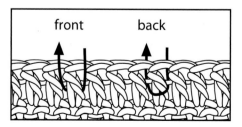